Cooking SCHOOL

Mexican Food

SARA GILBERT

CREATIVE EDUCATION & CREATIVE PAPERBACKS

Published by Creative Education and Creative Paperbacks
P.O. Box 227, Mankato, Minnesota 56002 • Creative Education
and Creative Paperbacks are imprints of The Creative Company
www.thecreativecompany.us

Design and production by Christine Vanderbeek
Printed in the United States of America

Photographs by Alamy (dbimages, John Elk III, Trevor Pearson),
Corbis (68/John Block/Ocean, John Block/Blend Images),
iStockphoto (DebbiSmirnoff, naelnabil), Shutterstock (area381,
bonchan, Igor Dutina, Jiri Hera, Vitaly Korovin, Dan Kosmayer,
Olga Miltsova, NEGOVURA, Sergey Nivens, pogonici, Evlakhov
Valeriy, Viktor1, VladislavGudovskiy, VolkOFF-ZS-BP, Valentyn
Volkov, Yganko), SuperStock (Cusp)

Library of Congress Cataloging-in-Publication Data
Gilbert, Sara. • Mexican food / by Sara Gilbert. • p. cm. —
(Cooking school) • *Summary*: An elementary introduction to the
relationship between cooking and Mexican culture, the effect of
local agriculture on the diets of different regions, common tools
such as rolling pins, and recipe instructions.
Includes bibliographical references
and index. • ISBN 978-1-60818-
504-7 (hardcover) • ISBN 978-
1-62832-098-5 (pbk)
1. Cooking, Mexican—
Juvenile literature. 2. Food—
Mexico—Juvenile literature. I. Title.
TX716.M4G53 2015
641.5972—dc23   2014002299

CCSS: RI.1.1, 2, 3, 5, 6, 7; RI.2.1,
2, 3, 5, 6, 7; RI.3.1, 3, 5, 7;
RF.1.1; RF.2.3, 4; RF.3.3

First Edition
9 8 7 6 5 4 3 2 1

Table of Contents

Fun Cooking

People everywhere have to cook. But cooking yummy, *nutritious* food can be fun. In Mexico, cooks have fun using *ingredients* that grow where they live.

In Mexico, people eat their main meal between 1 and 4 P.M.

Special Foods

Mexican food is an important part of the country's *culture*. Different foods are made for special holidays in Mexico. Many Mexican *recipes* use corn, beans, and chili peppers.

People make sugar skulls for the Day of the Dead holiday.

Chocolate grows in southern Mexico. People grind it with nuts, cinnamon, and spices to make a delicious drink.

Chocolate comes from cocoa beans.

11

In Mexico City, tacos and Mexican sand-wiches called *tortas* are sold in small shops on the busy streets.

Tacos can be made with beef, pork, chicken, or seafood.

On Mexico's Yucatán Peninsula, people use *tropical* fruits such as bitter oranges and mangoes to make a sauce called salsa.

The peppers and fruit in mango salsa make it spicy and sweet.

Tasty Tortillas

Corn tortillas are made with a tortilla press that flattens the dough between two pieces of metal or wood. Flour tortillas are made with a rolling pin.

Tacos

can be made with many different ingredients.

INGREDIENTS

1 pound ground beef

1 package taco seasoning

¾ cup water

diced tomatoes

lettuce

cheese

black olives

onions

corn or flour tortilla

DIRECTIONS

1. With an adult's help, brown 1 pound ground beef in a frying pan.

2. Add a package of taco seasoning and ¾ cup water and cook.

3. Prepare your taco toppings: diced tomatoes, lettuce, cheese, black olives, and onions.

4. Spoon some meat onto a corn or flour tortilla. Add your favorite toppings, and fold the taco shell around the fillings. Enjoy!

Salsa

can be served with chips or with tacos, burritos, or other meals.

INGREDIENTS

4 to 5 large tomatoes

1 small white onion

1 to 2 jalapeño peppers

fresh cilantro leaves

garlic

salt and pepper

1 tablespoon lemon juice

tortilla chips for serving

DIRECTIONS

1. Cut up 4 or 5 large tomatoes and a small white onion. If you like spicy salsa, cut up 1 or 2 jalapeño peppers—but be sure to wash your hands carefully after touching the peppers!

2. Mix everything in a bowl. Add fresh cilantro leaves, garlic, salt, and pepper. Stir in 1 tablespoon lemon juice.

3. Serve with tortilla chips.

Quesadillas

are usually made with tortillas and cheese.
But vegetables, beans, and meat can be used, too.

INGREDIENTS

2 flour tortillas

cheese

shredded chicken

onions

peppers

lettuce, salsa, and sour cream for topping

DIRECTIONS

1. Spray a frying pan with cooking spray, and heat the pan over medium heat.

2. Place a flour tortilla in the pan, then add cheese, shredded chicken, onions, peppers, or any other ingredients. Top with a second flour tortilla.

3. After about 1 minute, ask an adult to help you flip the quesadilla over. Let it cook for another minute.

4. Remove from the pan and cut into triangles. Top with lettuce, salsa, and sour cream!

Glossary

culture the artistic and social traditions of a group of people

ingredients any of the foods or liquids that combine to complete a recipe

nutritious healthy and good for you

recipes sets of instructions for making a certain dish, including a list of ingredients

tropical common in the geographic region known as the tropics

Read More

Blaxland, Wendy. *I Can Cook! Mexican Food.* Mankato, Minn.: Smart Apple Media, 2012.

Crocker, Betty. *Betty Crocker Kids Cook!* Minneapolis: Betty Crocker, 2007.

Low, Jennifer. *Kitchen for Kids.* New York: Whitecap Books, 2010.

Websites

http://www.pbs.org/food/theme/cooking-with-kids/
Find easy recipes to try by yourself or with an adult's assistance.

http://www.foodnetwork.com/cooking-with-kids/package/index.html
Learn to cook with celebrity chefs on the website of television's Food Network.

Index